DESTINY

Edwin Sánchez

BROADWAY PLAY PUBLISHING INC
New York
www.broadwayplaypublishing.com
info@broadwayplaypublishing.com

DESTINY
© Copyright 2022 Edwin Sánchez

First edition: September 2022
I S B N: 978-0-88145-936-4

Book design: Marie Donovan
Page make-up: Adobe InDesign
Typeface: Palatino

CHARACTERS & SETTING

DESTINY, *a transgender child, 12*
CUCA, *hir sister, 13*
ANDY, *the father, early 40s, very physical, Australian*
SONIA, *the mother, early 30s, Puerto Rican*
RENE, *late 40s, early 50s, blind*
JORGE, *a neighbor boy, 14, chubby*

New York

NOTE ON MUSIC

For performance of copyrighted songs, arrangements or recordings referenced in this play, permission of the copyright owner(s) must be obtained. Other songs, arrangements or recordings may be substituted provided permission from the copyright owner(s) of such songs, arrangements or recordings is obtained, or songs, arrangements or recordings in the public domain may be substituted.

ACT ONE

(Twelve year old DESTINY *enters hir parents' bedroom. Zie's in a bright tee shirt and jeans. Zie is small for hir age and wears hir hair on the longish side. At first glance you shouldn't be able to tell if zie's a boy or a girl. Zie goes to hir mother's vanity and sits. Zie looks at hir reflection in the mirror. Zie pulls hir hair up and tries to do a top knot. Zie gets some bobby pins and secures hir hair up. Hir hair is not really long enough for the style so it looks a bit off. Zie puts on some bangle bracelets and shakes hir wrists, smiling at the sound they make. Zie holds up a pair of earrings. Hir ears aren't pierced so zie can't wear them, but zie puts them over the top of hir ears. Looks at hirself.)*

DESTINY: Hello. My name is Destiny. It means meant to be. Like me. *(Zie takes out a long strand of brightly colored beads and winds them carefully around hir neck. Zie opens a bottle of perfume, smells it. Zie puts on a small dab on hir nose.)*

*(*DESTINY *stands, looks at hirself in the mirror and smiles. Suddenly hir sister,* CUCA, *13, not a tomboy but less feminine than* DESTINY *rushes in.)*

CUCA: Mami and Dada are parking! *(Seeing* DESTINY*)* What the fuck?!

*(*DESTINY *starts to quickly remove the earrings and the bangles.)*

DESTINY: I'm sorry. I'm sorry. Please.

CUCA: You said you were just gonna look at her stuff, Danny.

(CUCA *starts ripping bobby pins out of* DESTINY'*s hair.*)

DESTINY: Ow!

(CUCA *quickly looks out the window.*)

CUCA: They're coming up the stairs!

(*Everything is in hyper speed.* DESTINY *tries to unravel the necklace around hir neck, but can't.* CUCA *grabs at it almost choking hir.*)

DESTINY: Stop!! Stop it!!! You're choking me!!

(DESTINY *and* CUCA *hear the keys in the front door.* CUCA *stops.*)

CUCA: Sshh. Shit.

SONIA: (*From off stage*) Danny? Cuca?

(CUCA, *thinking quickly, pushes* DESTINY *to the ground and zie hides under hir parents bed as* SONIA *enters. Her look is retro. Tight clothing, a beehive hairstyle and heavy on the eye makeup.* CUCA *quickly tries to make it look like she was applying make up to herself.*)

CUCA: Surprise. Look how pretty I am.

SONIA: I told you not to play in my room. What's the matter with you.

CUCA: Sorry.

SONIA: Where's Danny?

CUCA: He went to get ice cream or something.

(SONIA *sees the disarray on her vanity.*)

SONIA: Look at this mess. You got to learn how to respect people's privacy.

CUCA: I'm sorry, mami. It's just that…sometimes I wanna look just like you.

SONIA: One of me is enough. Trust me. You made this mess, you clean it up. I'm gonna start cooking. And no dessert for you tonight.

(CUCA *nods as* SONIA *exits.*)

(DESTINY *slowly emerges from under the bed. Zie gently removes the necklace as* CUCA *begins to straighten up.*)

DESTINY: You can have my dessert. (*Zie tries to help.*) I'm sorry.

(CUCA *stops* DESTINY.)

CUCA: No you ain't sorry. Sometimes, it's like exhausting being your sister, you know? People get tired of taking care of you. Especially the people who love you. Especially when there's no end in sight.

(*Lights out on bedroom, up on living room where* SONIA *enters.* ANDY, *early 40s, big, muscular, sits, staring off. There is a punching bag set up in a corner of the living room.*)

SONIA: I'm gonna start dinner. You want anything special?

(*No answer*)

SONIA: I can…I can make whatever you want.

(SONIA *touches the back of* ANDY's *head. He takes her hand and kisses it.*)

SONIA: We got this, baby. We caught it early. It's gonna be easy breezy, japaneasy. You'll see.

(SONIA *exits. She begins to sing softly off stage.* ANDY *begins punching the bag.*)

(*Lights fade on* ANDY. *School bell. The sound effects of a loud inner city school flood the stage.*)

(*A shaft of light appears as if an entrance door has been pulled open. Through the shaft of light a defiant* CUCA [*"say something about my brother, come on!"*] *And a hopeful*

DESTINY *enter. The sound of the children in the background quickly fade. The silence is almost palpable. Zie has some colorful rubber bands on as bracelets and hir belt over hir long tee shirt, making it appear more like a dress than a shirt.* CUCA *grabs hir hand and looks out.* DESTINY *smiles. The school bell rings again. Muted voices return.)*

CUCA: I'll check with you after every class.

DESTINY: No, it's okay.

CUCA: Danny.

DESTINY: No, really. I think.

CUCA: Okay then. I'll meet you here after school. And don't go to the girls bathroom.

DESTINY: What if I have to go?

CUCA: Danny. Just hold it, okay? Till we get home.

(Second school bell is heard. CUCA *can't bring herself to leave* DESTINY.*)*

CUCA: This is my school. They know me here. Anybody give you any trouble you tell them you're my brother.

DESTINY: Sister.

CUCA: Humor me. Brother.

*(*DESTINY *looks down.)*

CUCA: No, no, it's okay. We'll play dolls when we get home, okay? Okay? But today you gotta be G I Joe, not Barbie. Just in school. You don't want people to hate on you, do you?

*(*DESTINY *shakes hir head "no".)*

CUCA: First day is always the hardest.

(The last bell. CUCA *stares at* DESTINY.*)*

CUCA: I gotta go. You'll be okay.

DESTINY: Can I have a Lifesaver?

(CUCA *gives* DESTINY *one.*)

CUCA: Okay. It's cherry. Please don't use it for lipstick.

(CUCA *runs off as* DESTINY *does precisely that, wetting the lifesaver and using it on hir lips.*)

(*The lights begin to darken on hir as the sound of hir heartbeat goes up. The sound of the children which was muted slowly turns to the rumble of a pack of dogs. Lights slowly out on* DESTINY.)

(*Lights up on* ANDY *and* SONIA. *He is dry heaving into a wastebasket. She stands beside him with a towel. In the background we hear faint sounds of street life. She rubs the back of his neck.*)

SONIA: Just breathe, baby.

ANDY: I'm trying. I want to throw up but nothing comes out.

(ANDY *continues to gasp for air. A truck horn is heard, summoning him.*)

SONIA: (*Calling out*) He'll be right out. (*To* ANDY) Just skip work today.

ANDY: No.

SONIA: Stubborn much?

ANDY: It's just the medicines fucking with me, that's all. You afraid?

SONIA: Nah.

ANDY: It's cancer, baby.

SONIA: Sshhh. Remember, easy breezy. You know what I say to cancer, right? (*She snaps her fingers, sings:*)
My boyfriend's back and there's gonna be trouble
Eya, eya my boyfriend's back
(*She kisses him.*)

ANDY: The guys are waiting.

SONIA: Let them wait. It's been a while.

(ANDY *and* SONIA *kiss again. She claps her hands and dances for him.*)

SONIA: Take me to heaven, baby. (*Sings*)
Eya, eya my boyfriend's back

(SONIA *kisses* ANDY *again. Truck horn is heard. She sits on him and they begin to kiss in earnest. Lights fade.*)

(*Lights up on* DESTINY *carrying hir lunch tray, hir knapsack on hir back. Zie goes to three different spots and it should be clear that no one lets hir sit with them.*)

DESTINY: Excuse me, could you move over a seat?

(*Nothing*)

DESTINY: So I can sit. Excuse me.

(*Still nothing.* DESTINY *walks to another table.*)

DESTINY: Hi, can I sit here?

(*Nothing.* DESTINY *goes to another table.*)

DESTINY: Hi, I'm just gonna eat.

(DESTINY *sits. Zie puts hir tray on the table and takes off hir knapsack and puts it next to hir. Zie looks up to see everyone who was sitting at hir table has left.*)

DESTINY: You don't have to go. Why is everybody going for?

(*Silence. A beat as* DESTINY *sits alone at the lunch room table. Zie reaches into hir knapsack and takes out a Bratz doll and sits her on the table.*)

DESTINY: Is this your first day? Mine, too.

(*Lights slowly fade. Lights up on* ANDY.)

ANDY: "What do you think I should do?" I ask my doctor. He looks at me and says, "It's spread". I look at Sonia

(SONIA *is lit in the background.*)

ANDY: Who looks straight at him. I can't read her at first, and when I squeeze her hand it becomes a claw that digs into my thigh.

SONIA: What is this, "it's spread, bullshit?"

ANDY: "Hasn't your husband kept you abreast?" And just like that my doctor throws me under the bus. "It's spread to his lymph nodes. We discussed this."

SONIA: How much?

ANDY: The doctor kindly answers, "How much time does your husband have or how much has it spread?"

SONIA: You know what I'm asking, mother fucker.

ANDY: The doctor shakes his head. Tells Sonia he's been treating me for over a year before he ever set eyes on her. Sonia exits to the elevator where I join her.

(ANDY *stands next to* SONIA. *Silence)*

ANDY: I'm sorry I got sick.

(SONIA *is silent.)*

ANDY: I said I'm sorry I got sick. I'm sorry I'm such a burden on you.

(SONIA *struggles to stay silent.)*

ANDY: I didn't do it on purpose. Look at me. I didn't do it on purpose.

SONIA: No, what you did on purpose was pretend it wasn't happening. Pick fights with me when your dick wouldn't work and hide that your balls and tits were hurting. That's what you did. You didn't want to be weak for me so you were this fake strong mother fucker who can't hide that he's dying anymore. Who's gonna leave me.

(SONIA *hits the elevator. She kicks it. She wants to hurt something.)*

ANDY: The elevator didn't lie to you. I did.

(Lights fade. Traffic sounds. CUCA *and* DESTINY *sit at the bus stop.)*

CUCA: Spread out. Put your bag next to you. I don't want no perv sitting next to us.

DESTINY: What's a perv?

CUCA: To some people, you.

DESTINY: Is it a good thing?

CUCA: Shut up. *(Silence)* Look, you can't keep waiting for me after detention. You gotta come home when they make me stay.

DESTINY: I don't mind.

CUCA: And it's your fault I got detention.

*(*DESTINY *puts hir head on* CUCA*'s shoulder.)*

CUCA: I see you do it again tomorrow, I'ma bust you up. Crack your head wide open. *(She kisses hir on the forehead.)* Watch all the crazy spill out.

DESTINY: You think I'm crazy?

CUCA: You ain't normal. That's for damn sure. That's our bus. Come on.

*(*DESTINY *doesn't move.* CUCA *gently touches hir face.)*

CUCA: You feel like you gonna cry?

*(*DESTINY *nods.)*

CUCA: We'll wait for the next one. I shouldn't a said that. You as normal as you can be.

DESTINY: Do you hate me? I mean you get into fights and detention cause of me. Do you hate me?

CUCA: No. Not yet.

(Lights fade. A boxing ring "ding" is heard. Lights up on living room, where ANDY'S *punching bag hangs.* CUCA *puts on her father's boxing gloves and begins to punch the bag.)*

(Hard. Harder)

(A knock. CUCA *opens the door to* JORGE, *a chubby boy of 14.)*

JORGE: Hello, I'm Jorge from Jorge, Inc.

CUCA: Wait, what?

JORGE: Jorge Incorporated is a new and exciting full service, do anything firm.

CUCA: Uh huh.

JORGE: We specialize in everything and our rates are reasonable.

CUCA: Goodbye. *(She tries to close the door.)*

JORGE: No, wait, take a card. *(Offering her a card)*

CUCA: And you're gonna guess which one?

JORGE: It's my business card!

CUCA: No, this says Delgado Plumbing. You Delgado?

JORGE: No.

CUCA: More like Delgordo.

JORGE: Delgado went outta business, he gave me his business cards.

CUCA: So you a plumber?

JORGE: Turn the card over.

*(*CUCA *does.)*

CUCA: Jorge, Inc.

(Stand off.)

JORGE: Maybe your moms needs something done. Change lightbulbs, run errands.

CUCA: I do that.

JORGE: Help her move stuff.

CUCA: My father does that.

JORGE: Okay then.

(*Silence*)

CUCA: So leave.

JORGE: So gimme back my card.

(CUCA *doesn't.* JORGE *doesn't leave.*)

CUCA: You're in Mrs Buchwalter's home room?

JORGE: Yeah.

CUCA: Seventh grade?

JORGE: Sixth. I got left back.

CUCA: That's no big deal. ...I'm in Mrs Spelling's class.

JORGE: I know. You're famous. You're father's Australian. You ever been?

CUCA: To Australia? Once. When I was a baby. Don't remember shit. (*Correcting herself*) Nothing. I should keep the card in case we need something.

JORGE: Yeah, okay. I could come back and check in a couple of days.

CUCA: You don't have to.

JORGE: I know.

CUCA: I mean, you wrote your number on the card. I could just call you.

JORGE: But you won't.

CUCA: You don't know that. What you wanna make money for?

JORGE: I'm the man of the house. I polish shoes, too. You got any shoes?

CUCA: Do we have any shoes? That's so stupid.

JORGE: You make me nervous.

CUCA: Why? I'm not gonna beat you up.

JORGE: But you could. …And you're pretty and shit. Gimme back the card, you ain't gonna call.

(CUCA *gives* JORGE *back the card.*)

CUCA: You so crazy.

(JORGE *leaves. Lights out. Later.* ANDY *and* SONIA *enter. He takes off his leather jacket, goes to hang it on a hook and misses. He picks up the jacket and angrily throws it against the wall.*)

SONIA: Oh yeah, teach that jacket a lesson. I'm gonna make some coffee.

ANDY: No, I gotta start a diary for the kids. Film me.

SONIA: Not now.

ANDY: Yes now. While I can still remember everything.

(SONIA *takes out her phone and films him.*)

SONIA: Okay, just don't scare them.

ANDY: I'm informing them.

SONIA: "What it's like to die in slow motion?"

ANDY: It ain't slow, baby. You'll be a widow by the end of the year.

(SONIA *drops the phone.*)

ANDY: I wasn't forthright with you. I want the kids to have this.

(SONIA *picks up the phone. Films*)

ANDY: Andy Caldwell here, your dada. Chapter one. So doctor says it's no bueno.

SONIA: Now suddenly you know Spanish?

ANDY: In fact I am jodido.

SONIA: *(Half laughs)* Shut up.

ANDY: My testicular cancer is moving a lo pronto.

SONIA: I'ma a hit you. I swear to God I'ma hit you.

ANDY: So your mami, who is a hot mami.

SONIA: Don't make me laugh, cabron.

ANDY: Is…so beautiful. Still. Even when she hides her face from me to cry. She's gonna be a beautiful widow.

(SONIA *puts the phone down.*)

ANDY: We're making a diary here, baby. For the kids.

SONIA: No.

ANDY: What do you mean "no"?

SONIA: I ain't gonna be no widow. Fuck that. Fuck you, fuck cancer.

ANDY: Yes to all of it. But you gotta film me. I gotta leave them something. Just in case.

(SONIA *once again begins to film.*)

ANDY: So I want to explain to both of you what I have. There are gonna be people who will try to and I think they're just gonna scare you. Not on purpose you know, but. Do your dada a favor and never google images of testicular cancer, okay? So, if you're seeing this, it's cause I'm gone. Danny, Cuca… My balls are me. And I was gonna make them work. I was not about to allow them to be weak. I muscled through. I worked twice as hard, lifted more than any of my guys. Didn't wince once. That's the trick, I thought. You bully your body. The inside and the outside. You tell it what to do, how much, if any, pain it can feel. This is how we Caldwell men are, Danny. Tough as nails, but…I wasn't very fair to your mami.

(SONIA *stops filming.*)

ANDY: They need to hear this, so when they remember you being angry for no reason they'll know why. Mamita, when you can't take it anymore, just take the kids and leave. It won't change how I feel about you.

(Lights out. Later that night. Lights up on CUCA *and* DESTINY's *room. Enter* SONIA, *who is a bit drunk. On amaretto. It is late.* CUCA *is under her sheet. We see the glow from her cell phone screen.)*

SONIA: Hey.

*(*CUCA *quickly puts her phone away.)*

CUCA: What's the matter, mami?

SONIA: Nothing. Can't a mother say hey. Shh, let's not wake up Danny. It's just us girls.

*(*CUCA *watches her* SONIA.*)*

SONIA: I should get you more dolls. You need more dolls.

CUCA: Okay.

SONIA: Danny looks like Dada, right? You want a taste of amaretto?

CUCA: Sure.

*(*SONIA *passes her glass to* CUCA.*)*

SONIA: Not too much.

CUCA: It tastes a little like medicine.

SONIA: Sweet medicine though, right?

CUCA: Yeah.

SONIA: Move over.

CUCA: You fight with dada?

SONIA: No. And what do you know about that? You don't know shit. He's sick, you know. And sad all the time.

CUCA: He'll get better.

SONIA: *(Drinks)* Your Dada is very virile. It's almost the same word in Spanish. Look it up. Not macho. Macho's stupid, you know, always gotta be proving, trying to make someone else feel like less so they can feel like more. No, your Dada had "man" tattooed on him from the day I met him.

(SONIA *offers* CUCA *more amaretto, who drinks.*)

CUCA: This is nice.

SONIA: He's still a young man, well youngish, but he can't perform anymore.

CUCA: Okay, I'm going to sleep now.

SONIA: So, …I'm lonely. I'm supposed to have friends I talk to about this, but I got no friends. I just have my little family. That's all I ever needed. We should do this again. Only you should dress up. I'll put makeup on you. You'd like that, right?

CUCA: Is dada gonna die?

SONIA: I shouldn't be talking to you but I have nobody else.

CUCA: What am I supposed to do with what you tell me?

SONIA: Just listen.

CUCA: After I listen, mami, who do I talk to?

(SONIA *begins to cry.*)

(*She exits.*)

SONIA: You're a kid. You should be sleeping.

(*Later. Living room.* DESTINY *is in front of the punching bag which is about the same size as zie. Zie begins to hum to hirself. Zie smiles and begins to dance with the punching bag.* ANDY *enters, takes hir in for a moment.*)

(DESTINY *notices, stops dancing. Awkward silence*)

ANDY: I used to dance with your mami all the time. Is there a little girl you want to take dancing?

DESTINY: No.

ANDY: You sure?

(DESTINY *is silent.*)

ANDY: How was school?

DESTINY: Okay.

(ANDY *puts* DESTINY *is a gentle headlock and kisses the top of hir head.*)

ANDY: ...Throw a punch at me.

(DESTINY *just stares at* ANDY.)

ANDY: It's in good fun. See, you use your right hand to protect your face and jab with your left. C'mon.

(ANDY *begins sparring with* DESTINY.)

DESTINY: *(Calling out to* SONIA*)* Mami.

(SONIA *enters.*)

ANDY: No, no, no, just us two guys. I gotta make sure you can defend yourself. Don't look at her, look at me. C'mon, it's fun.

(ANDY *playfully jabs at* DESTINY *who puts both hands up to defend hirself. He grabs hir hand with his own and hits himself with it.*)

Hit me. C'mon, hit your old man. Hit me.

SONIA: Andy, ya basta.

ANDY: He's gotta know how to defend himself. You hit, you follow through. If someone comes at you, you knock them out. That's the only language a bully understands.

(ANDY *again hits himself with* DESTINY's *hand. He staggers back, overacting his reaction to the punch. Zie pulls hir hand back.*)

ANDY: Wow. You really got me with that one. That's my boy.

(*Later.* CUCA *storms in to the front stoop, a sheepish*
DESTINY *follows, carrying some Italian ices, still in their*
containers. Zie gives them to her.)

DESTINY: Here, hold them up against your hand.

(CUCA *angrily throws them on the street.* DESTINY *picks*
them up, holds them out to her. After a beat she takes them
and holds them against her knuckles.)

(*Silence*)

DESTINY: I'll tell them it was my fault.

CUCA: Just shut up. Don't say nothing.
Why'd you take mami's lipstick to school?

DESTINY: You told me to shut up.

CUCA: Why?!

DESTINY: It's pretty.

CUCA: On her it's pretty.

DESTINY: I didn't put it on.

CUCA: No, but it rolled out of your knapsack and when
you went for it Junior saw it.

DESTINY: It's none of his business.

CUCA: It's not my business either but I had to bust him
in the mouth when he came at you. I'm the one who
got suspended and I'm not gonna be in school for a
week to look after your freak ass.

DESTINY: Don't call me that.

CUCA: I stick up for you, I can call you whatever I like.
Junior had to be a bleeder.

DESTINY: Yeah, you hit him hard. How's your hand?

(CUCA *glares at* DESTINY.)

DESTINY: What are they gonna tell mami and da?

(CUCA *and* DESTINY *sit on the stoop.*)

CUCA: They're gonna call them to the school. Have a meeting with the Principal and Junior's parents. And da's gonna have to hear about the lipstick. And he's gotta take it and not blink while Junior and his father smirk at him and tell him boys will be boys. You gotta stop being so selfish. Dada's sick.

DESTINY: I know.

CUCA: Then act like it.

DESTINY: It's not easy being my sister, is it?

CUCA: Oh, it's cake. For a week you're on your own. You take the side streets and if you see kids from the school duck into a store.

DESTINY: Can't you pick me up?

CUCA: No, you gotta learn there's a price to being you. You gotta learn to be invisible.

(DESTINY *looks down.*)

CUCA: What else you got in the bag?

DESTINY: Nothing.

CUCA: Don't make me look.

DESTINY: A doll.

CUCA: Why?

DESTINY: Cause she makes me feel like me.

CUCA: Come on. They probably got the call by now. It's not always about you, you know.

DESTINY: What are we gonna do?

CUCA: We are gonna convince mami that they don't need to go. I'll make up some story. Mami's only half there now anyways. You better pray there's amaretto in the house.

(*Later.* SONIA *sits in front of her vanity. No make up. An open tube of eye liner in her hand. The weight of the world*

*on her shoulders. She listens to something like Carmita
Jimenez's Papeles on the radio.)*

SONIA: I can't create me. I can't fake it anymore.
Not the way you want to see me. *(She puts down the
eyeliner.)*

ANDY: Yes you can.

SONIA: No. I can't. I wasn't born with eyeliner, you
know. I had to learn how to apply. And I'm tired.

ANDY: Why don't we skip the doctor today?

SONIA: You didn't sleep last night, you threw up lunch.
We're going.

ANDY: Well you're not gonna go like that, are you?

SONIA: Ay Andy, no jodas.

ANDY: *(Laughs)* That's my girl. Now you gotta look like
my girl.

SONIA: I'm not a girl. Not anymore.

ANDY: That's right. You're my queen.

SONIA: See, when you play that card you always win.

*(SONIA returns her gaze to her reflection in her mirror.
Throughout ANDY's monologue she will apply her very
elaborate eye make up.)*

ANDY: You walk in and you stop a room cold. You
always do. All eyes on you. That beautiful artifice on
the outside and that sweet marshmallow filling. You're
my Achilles heel, you know that. When I can't sleep I
still know I'm lying next to you, and that's enough. I
think about how your natural scent always made me
hard. How when you sweat you glow like an opal.
And I love when you curse in Spanish, always makes
me laugh. Such a beautiful red mouth saying those
nasty things. And me laughing would just make you
curse some more. Never met anybody who could

curse like you, man or woman. My lady with the cat eyes. Yeah, make 'em bigger. My ma liked you straight away, thought you looked like the girl groups of her youth. She liked that you were tough. That you weren't afraid of my being a behemoth. "That's the girl that'll tame you, my boy!" she said to me.

(SONIA *sits staring at her Amy Winehouse-like reflection. An open tube of lipstick in her hand*)

SONIA: *(Whispers)* Don't die on me.

ANDY: What color you got there.

SONIA: Black red. *(She puts on the lipstick, blots. She draws a beauty mark by her mouth.)*

ANDY: You are giving me life, mujercita.

(ANDY *stands behind* SONIA *touching her shoulders, puts his face next to hers. She draws a beauty mark by his mouth. He laughs, she kisses it away. She takes a napkin to wipe away her kiss print.*)

ANDY: Don't. I want to wear you today.

(*Street. Pedestrian island with a park bench.* RENE, *late 40s early 50s sits reading her braille book. The sound of traffic is at full then fades to a dull background noise.*)

(DESTINY *runs on to the sound of a car braking suddenly. Traffic resumes as an out of breath zie looks out into the traffic that just missed hir.*)

RENE: Hey, you okay?

(DESTINY *nods.*)

RENE: Honey, I'm blind, yes or no.

DESTINY: I'm okay.

RENE: It just missed you.

(DESTINY *gets near* RENE, *having never actually seen a blind person face to face, and waves a hand in front of her face.*)

RENE: Hello to you too.

(DESTINY *jumps back.*)

RENE: Relax. I felt your breath. You smell nice. What is that? Lilac?

DESTINY: My mother's soap.

RENE: Does she know you use it?

DESTINY: …Yes…

RENE: I love it when children lie. What are you, ten, eleven?

DESTINY: Twelve.

RENE: What a pretty girl you must be.

DESTINY: You wanna feel my face?

RENE: You must watch a lot of television, don't you?

(RENE *feels* DESTINY's *face.*)

RENE: Very pretty.

DESTINY: My hair is brown and really shiny and it bounces when I walk. (*Zie sees some classmates and gets closer to* RENE.)

RENE: You scared? (*Silence*) Are you nodding?

DESTINY: No, I'm not scared.

RENE: Some kids? Sit by me. I have a cane. I know how to use it.

(DESTINY *sits.* RENE *picks up her cane.*)

RENE: Which way?

DESTINY: To your right.

(RENE *waves her cane menacingly in that direction.*)

RENE: They ask you, tell them I'm your grandmother.

DESTINY: Wait? You a woman?

RENE: Don't be fresh. …They're gone now.

DESTINY: Yeah. How could you tell?

RENE: Your breathing changed. You can go now.

DESTINY: I...I was going to a party.

RENE: That's nice. *(Tries to go back to her book)*

DESTINY: It is. And I have long hair.

RENE: Oh I could tell.

DESTINY: You could?

RENE: Uh huh. My name is Rene Ramirez. You see me again you can call me Miss Rene.

DESTINY: My name is Destiny.

RENE: That's a pretty name.

DESTINY: I know, right. I'm a pretty girl.

RENE: You know someone else is supposed to say that, right?

DESTINY: Oh. I should go.

RENE: You don't want to be late to your party.

DESTINY: No.

RENE: Bye.

DESTINY: Bye. *(Zie gets up.)*

RENE: Hey Destiny. You are a very pretty girl.

DESTINY: You're pretty too.

RENE: Am I?

(DESTINY sits back down.)

DESTINY: Oh yeah. What are you reading?

RENE: *The Hunchback of Notre Dame.* In French. I can read over a dozen languages in braille.

DESTINY: Wow.

RENE: You see that penthouse up there? The tallest building on the corner? That's where I live. With too many servants. I come here to get away from everybody. *(Laughs)* It's always, Miss Rene can I get you some tea? Miss Rene are you comfortable. I like being by myself now and then, don't you?

(DESTINY smiles and nods.)

RENE: If you're nodding I can't see it.

(DESTINY laughs.)

RENE: No one bothers you when you're alone.

DESTINY: Yes. Maybe I'll see you again.

RENE: Maybe you will.

DESTINY: What do you think I look like?

RENE: Well, you told me. You're a very pretty girl.

(Lights out, up on ANDY opening the door to JORGE.)

JORGE: Hello, Cuca.

ANDY: Do I look like Cuca? You better answer quick.

JORGE: No sir.

ANDY: Why are you coming here for my daughter?

(CUCA enters.)

JORGE: I'm not coming here for your daughter.
Hi Cuca.

CUCA: Go ahead, Jorge. This is your chance.

JORGE: Hello, I'm Jorge, from Jorge Inc. I'm here as a small business man, who very much like yourself, is the C E O and president of my company.

ANDY: What's he saying?

CUCA: Show him your card.

JORGE: I forgot them.

ANDY: Well good day and good luck. *(About to close the door)*

JORGE: I do things. Anything you need, I do.

ANDY: You're an errand boy?

JORGE: No. Yes.

ANDY: Gopher? You know, go for this, go for that?

JORGE: …Yes. (*Looking straight at* CUCA) I'm anything you need me to be.

ANDY: We don't need anything. (*He closes the door on* JORGE.)

JORGE: (*From behind the closed door*) I'll be back tomorrow, Mr uh, Austrailian.

ANDY: Well, at least Boy Boobs is polite.

CUCA: Don't call him that!

(ANDY *makes kissy face sounds as he walks off.*)

(*Later.* ANDY *and* DESTINY *by the punching bag. There is a huge stuffed bear between them. It is almost as big as zie.*)

ANDY: You like him?

DESTINY: It's not my birthday.

ANDY: No, but I thought you'd like a friend. A buddy. (*In a bearlike voice*) Hi Danny, I'm— (*In regular voice*) Pick a name.

DESTINY: Cindy.

ANDY: A boy's name. Jack. That's his name. Look at him throw a punch. (*He moves the bear as if it were hitting the punching bag.*) See? Now you try it.

(DESTINY *tries to move the bear the same way* ANDY *did.*)

DESTINY: Thank you.

ANDY: You're gonna be taller than me when you grow up. Stronger, too. Gonna rename the company Caldwell and Son. What do you think about that?

(DESTINY *exits with bear.* JORGE *enters with* CUCA.)

ANDY: *(To* JORGE*)* Hold the bag for me.

(JORGE *holds the punching bag as* ANDY *begins pummeling the bag. He is really wailing on the bag.)*

ANDY: Hey boy boobs, you a hard worker?

JORGE: Yes, sir.

ANDY: You want a job?

(Lights down. Up on CUCA *and* DESTINY *playing dolls.)*

DESTINY: Let's play fashion show.

CUCA: No. Okay. But this time mine gets to be the fashion model.

DESTINY: They can both be models.

CUCA: No. Yours has gotta be the photographer.

DESTINY: You can't always be the model.

CUCA: Then I don't want to play.

(CUCA *and* DESTINY *brush their respective dolls hair. Silence)*

CUCA: I'm gonna look like mami when I grow up.

DESTINY: Me too.

CUCA: No. You're gonna look like da.

DESTINY: I don't want to look like da, I want to look like mami.

CUCA: You won't.

DESTINY: Why?

CUCA: Cause. Someday I'll have a chest like mami and you'll have a chest like da.

(Silence. DESTINY *suddenly hits* CUCA *with the doll.)*

CUCA: Ow!

(CUCA *hits* DESTINY *back. Silence)*

CUCA: Da's gonna take you for a haircut today.

DESTINY: I want long hair, like you.

CUCA: Too bad.

(DESTINY *hits* CUCA *with the doll again.*)

CUCA: Ow! Quit doing that.

DESTINY: How come you have hair under your arms?

CUCA: It's just a little.

DESTINY: How come?

CUCA: Girls get hair in places. Boys get hair too. In different places.

DESTINY: Some night when you're sleeping I'm gonna cut all your hair off. (*Kisses the doll, brushes the doll's hair.*)

CUCA: Even the hair on my head?

DESTINY: Especially the hair on your head.

CUCA: Still won't make you a girl.

(DESTINY *goes to hit* CUCA *again with the doll but she stops the doll midway.*)

CUCA: Nothing will. Nothing. You have a pee pee. You're a boy.

(DESTINY *looks down, brushes the dolls hair and begins to cry quietly.*)

CUCA: It's not my fault. …Okay, yours can be the model.

(*Later.* ANDY *and* SONIA*'s bedroom. She sits on the bed smoking. He enters.*)

ANDY: Since when do you smoke?

SONIA: She didn't smoke. The Sonia before everything went to shit didn't smoke. I'm not her anymore.

(ANDY *gently takes the cigarette from* SONIA'*s hand. She takes it back, forcefully, looks at him, like she's about to burn him, stops herself. She puts the cigarette out on the vanity.*)

SONIA: That Sonia had everything and didn't know it. Healthy husband, some money in the bank.

ANDY: I'm gonna start working again and my crew is still doing moves.

SONIA: Normal kids.

ANDY: Our kids are fine.

SONIA: Cuca's fine.

ANDY: Danny's fine.

(SONIA *tries to relight the stubbed out cigarette, can't. She looks at the flame from the lighter.*)

(*She throws the lighter across the room.*)

SONIA: Did you not have your balls removed cause of me?

ANDY: No, cause of me. I didn't want to live that way. Gonna leave you alone for a while.

SONIA: Yeah okay. If I had to have a double mastectomy would you stop loving me?

ANDY: Of course not.

(*Next day*)

(CUCA *and* DESTINY *rush in from outside. She is carrying a dress box.*)

CUCA: It came! It came!

SONIA: What came?

DESTINY: Her communion dress! Just like the picture!!! It has flowers and lace.

CUCA: Hey! It's my dress! Flowers and lace and ribbons! It has a veil.

(ANDY *enters.*)

DESTINY: It has a veil!!!

CUCA: I'm gonna try it on.

SONIA: No, you're sweaty. You can't/

ANDY: She wants to see herself in it.

SONIA: /put it on. No! When does my no matter in this goddamn house! I said no!!

(CUCA *starts to cry. She throws the dress box on the floor.*)

ANDY: Hey. Hey, you know what you need? White patent leather shoes. Come on. Let's go get 'em.

(ANDY *takes* CUCA *by the hand and exits.* SONIA *picks up the dress box.*)

DESTINY: It's really pretty.

(SONIA *turns on the stereo, looks for some loud salsa music, blares it. She begins to dance by herself.*)

SONIA: Come on, baby. Dance with mami.

DESTINY: Mami, it's loud.

SONIA: Dance with me.

(SONIA *pulls* DESTINY *to her and begins to dance with hir. Zie is trying.*)

SONIA: Dance like a boy.

(DESTINY *tries to butch up hir dancing, but zie is imitating* SONIA'*s movements.*)

SONIA: C'mon, dance like you're a boy!

(DESTINY *breaks free and runs to hir room.* SONIA *raises the volume and keeps dancing. She begins to cry*).

(*Street.* ANDY *and* CUCA. *She carries a shoebox. She is eating an ice cream cone.*)

(*They stop.*)

ANDY: Nothing better than Mr Softee.

CUCA: You think I'm fat, dada?

ANDY: You? Who told you that? You are perfect.
See those boys over there? They are trying to be so
stealth, but they are of a mind to open that fire hydrant.

CUCA: They can't. There's a lock on it. I saw the city
put it on.

ANDY: Now why they wanna do that for? Especially on
a hot day like today.

(ANDY *and* CUCA *watch the boys trying to open the
hydrant.*)

CUCA: …How sick are you?

ANDY: Who said I'm sick?

CUCA: Just tell me so I'll know, that's all.

(ANDY *stares at* CUCA *for a moment. He gets on the ground
and starts doing push ups.*)

ANDY: Count 'em off.

CUCA: Dada, we're in the middle of the street.

ANDY: One! Two! Three!

(CUCA *looks around at everyone looking at* ANDY.)

CUCA: *(Proudly)* Oh yeah! That's my father. He's doing
push ups! *(She begins to count them off.)*

ANDY: Sit on my back. Let's really give them a show!

(*As* CUCA *does, lights shift to* SONIA *who lights a candle
and crosses herself. She addresses a crucifix.*)

SONIA: You deaf? Or just angry at us? Which one is it?

(*We hear the sound of a toilet flushing. Having just thrown
up,* ANDY *enters in baggy pajama bottoms and a stained tee
shirt.*)

ANDY: Can't keep nothing down.

(SONIA *hands* ANDY *a glass of water and a bottle of pills.*)

ANDY: Sit with me a bit.

SONIA: Gotta clean the bathroom. Don't want the kids to see it like that.

ANDY: They're sleeping.

SONIA: Wish I was.

ANDY: Sorry I'm an inconvenience.

SONIA: I'm sorry you decided to play quien es mas macho with your little girl.

ANDY: …I did fifty.

SONIA: I don't care.

ANDY: Used to be able to do a hundred. Two hundred easy. Used to be able to make love to you for hours.

(SONIA *takes a face towel and gently wipes* ANDY's *face. She tries to kiss him.*)

ANDY: Don't. Won't lead to nothing.

SONIA: Maybe I just want you to hold me.

ANDY: And do what? I can't do anything.

SONIA: …Tomorrow's chemo. Take your pills, don't take 'em. I don't care.

ANDY: I wish you didn't care.

SONIA: Don't worry, I'm getting there.

(*Later.* DESTINY *holds up* CUCA's *communion dress.*)

DESTINY: You should get a special hanger for this.

CUCA: What for? I'm only gonna wear it once.

DESTINY: Can I have it when you're done?

CUCA: Danny, you know mami and dada are not gonna let you have my dress.

DESTINY: But if you give it to me.

CUCA: No way. They won't.

DESTINY: What if I hide it?

CUCA: And do what with it?

DESTINY: Just look at it.

CUCA: Gimme the dress. I gotta put it away.

DESTINY: Are your hands clean?

CUCA: It's my fucking dress.

(DESTINY *hands the dress to* CUCA.)

DESTINY: Is dada sick?

CUCA: He told me no.

DESTINY: Do you believe him?

CUCA: I'm gonna hang my dress in the center, between your clothes and mine. And after my communion I'ma leave it right there. Every time you look at it, know that it's yours.

DESTINY: How sick is he?

CUCA: Da wouldn't lie.

(*Later. The park bench*)

(DESTINY *sits holding a plastic bag. From the bag zie takes out* CUCA's *communion dress and places it over hirself as if wearing it.*)

RENE: I brought you something.

DESTINY: I'm not allowed to take things from strangers. Didn't they teach you that growing up?

RENE: And you shouldn't. But I'm not asking you to get in a car with me.

DESTINY: Wait. You drive?

RENE: Just airplanes. (*She takes a bejeweled barrette out of her pocket.*) I used to wear it, back in the day.

DESTINY: When you were a girl?

RENE: I'm still a girl. Just an old one. Oh and blind. And truth be told my knees aren't what they used to be.

(DESTINY *takes the barrette.*)

DESTINY: It's beautiful.

RENE: They're real diamonds.

DESTINY: Are they?

RENE: Of course. People always give me jewelry.

DESTINY: I'm going to share it with my sister. She shares all her things with me.

RENE: She's a good sister. Put the barrette on. Let me feel it.

(DESTINY *clips the barrette on the top of hir head, takes* RENE's *hand and puts it on top of it.*)

DESTINY: I don't like nobody touching my hair.

RENE: I'm the same way. Did school let out already or is it Saturday? Sometimes days blend to me.

DESTINY: Saturday. I'm wearing a pretty dress.

RENE: Oh. Are you going to another party?

DESTINY: Yeah. It's a tea party. You can touch the dress.

(RENE *does.*)

RENE: It feels so soft.

DESTINY: It has flowers all over it. It looks pretty on me.

RENE: I'm sure it does.

DESTINY: Yes. I have to go to my party. I have a lot of friends, just like you, but I wanted to show you my dress first. I don't mean show.

RENE: I know what you mean.

(DESTINY *rises, letting the dress brush against* RENE.)

DESTINY: Could you ever see?

RENE: A long time ago.

DESTINY: What happened?

RENE: Bye bye Destiny.

(DESTINY *reaches over and holds* RENE'*s hand.*)

DESTINY: ...I feel safe.

(*A camera clicks. A still life picture comes to life.*)

(CUCA, *in her white communion dress and veil stands holding a bouquet in her hands. At her side is* DESTINY *in a suit. She smiles in the picture, zie does not.*)

SONIA: It's her communion. She's supposed to be the only one in the picture. It's bad enough we made her wait until she was thirteen!

ANDY: But he looks so nice in his suit. Like a little man.

SONIA: It looks like our children are getting married. To each other.

ANDY: The things that come outta your mouth.

(*Later.* CUCA *sits in her communion outfit.* ANDY *is crouching on the floor in front of her, feeding her ice cream from a bowl.*)

CUCA: I look pretty, huh?

ANDY: You look like ice cream. Very pretty.

SONIA: She's gonna get that dress dirty. Go get changed.

ANDY: Mami's a pill today. (*Pointing to* CUCA'*s dress*) See, no mess.

CUCA: Mami, I look pretty, right.

SONIA: You look like me, so yeah, you look pretty. You want whip cream?

CUCA: Yes please.

(DESTINY *enters, no more suffocating suit, just jeans and a brightly colored tee shirt.*)

SONIA: Why'd you change?

(DESTINY *shrugs.*)

ANDY: Next time I see you like this you'll be a bride.

CUCA: Don't ruin the ice cream moment, da.

ANDY: Why you gotta look like your mother?

(SONIA *gives* DESTINY *a bowl of ice cream who ignores it and continues staring at* ANDY *lovingly feeding ice cream to* CUCA.)

ANDY: What do you wanna do today? It's your day.

(CUCA *looks at* SONIA.)

SONIA: Yeah, it's your day. What's left of it.

CUCA: I don't know.

DESTINY: We can go to the Botanical Gardens.

(*Everyone suddenly looks at* DESTINY.)

DESTINY: I mean, if you want.

SONIA: (*To* DESTINY) Eat your ice cream before it melts.

CUCA: The Botanical Gardens is good. But I just wanna go with da.

SONIA: Why not me?

CUCA: Only if you both don't fight.

ANDY: We never fight. She just goes from zero to Puerto Rican at warp speed.

SONIA: You wanna wear that ice cream, pendejo?

(SONIA *and* ANDY *laugh.*)

DESTINY: You don't hate each other, right?

SONIA: No baby, of course not. That's just how we talk.

CUCA: You don't ever sound like you love each other.

ANDY: Parents just go through things, that's all. We love each other, right?

SONIA: Right pendejo.

ANDY: *(To* CUCA*)* You got a little scuff on your shoe.

SONIA: Take them off. I'll clean them.

*(*ANDY *take off* CUCA*'s shoes.)*

DESTINY: I'll clean them.

*(*CUCA *stares as* DESTINY *exits with her shoes.)*

ANDY: More ice cream Yeah. Chocolate this time.

SONIA: She's wearing white, dummy. Vanilla.

ANDY: She talks like that to everybody. The day she doesn't, that's when you have to worry.

(Outside, lights up on DESTINY *trying to squeeze a foot in* CUCA*'s shoes. Zie stands on hir toes in the shoes and walks to hir bedroom.* ANDY *and* CUCA *can be heard laughing through the door.)*

ANDY: Try it again.

CUCA: G'day, matey!

ANDY: Bigger.

CUCA: G'day matey!!!

SONIA: You two are idiots.

*(*SONIA *exits to their laughter carrying a bowl of more ice cream for* DESTINY*. She sees hir shoes on the floor.)*

(Later)

ANDY: *(Films himself)* Hey, Dada here. Chapter who knows. Today's a good day. Got some strength, kept food down, almost had an erection. I'll delete that later. Easily better than the last few days. So I'm gonna treasure you all a little bit more. Today I feel lucky.

(Later. Living Room)

ANDY: *(Calling out)* Danny? Where's Danny?

SONIA: Hiding. He can sense when you're gonna take him to the barber.

(A knock. SONIA *opens the door to* JORGE.*)*

SONIA: I can take him later.

ANDY: Nah, I want to show him off.

JORGE: Good morning Mrs Caldwell, good morning Mr Caldwell.

ANDY: Just Andy is fine.

JORGE: I finished moving the boxes in the truck, so there's plenty of room now for the next move.

SONIA: *(To* ANDY*)* You got another move? I thought your crew was/

ANDY: Just me and the boy. *(To* JORGE*)* Your hair's a little scraggly there.

JORGE: Yes Mr Andy.

ANDY: I'll take you to my barber. *(Calls out)* Danny!

SONIA: Danny! Carajo, hello?!

ANDY: *(To* JORGE*)* Don't your mother send you to the barber?

*(*CUCA *enters.)*

JORGE: She's got other things on her plate. And my father's gone, you know.

ANDY: I know and I didn't ask you.

JORGE: Yes Mr Andy.

ANDY: *(To* SONIA*)* Go find Danny.

CUCA: Hey Jorge.

SONIA: *(To* CUCA*)* Go find Danny.

CUCA: Bye Jorge. *(She exits.)*

ANDY: You look all flustered when you see my daughter. Stop it.

(CUCA *enters her parent's bedroom. She goes directly to the bed and crouches next to it.*)

CUCA: Five minutes more and he'll be gone.

DESTINY: *(Voice only)* Good.

CUCA: He's gonna cut your hair hisself if you keep hiding. Danny? D?

DESTINY: I heard you. Is he very mad?

CUCA: No. I think he's taking Jorge instead.

DESTINY: Oh. Okay. (*Zie emerges from under the bed.*) Da likes Jorge, right?

CUCA: He can't stand him. I think.

(CUCA *exits.* DESTINY *shakes the dust bunnies off. Standing, half hidden by the bed and facing the mirror on the vanity, zie removes hir shirt, lowers hir pants and underwear. Zie stares at hir reflection.*)

(SONIA *enters.*)

DESTINY: *(To the reflection)* Why are you so ugly?

SONIA: Niño, get dressed.

(*A very embarrassed* DESTINY *gets dressed.*)

SONIA: I mean, I've seen it all before, I made it for Christ's sake, well half of it anyway.

(SONIA *sits on the bed,* DESTINY *sits next to her and puts hir head in her lap.*)

SONIA: C'mere. Your hair is too long.

DESTINY: Uh uh.

SONIA: One more week.

DESTINY: Mami, you like cutting your hair?

SONIA: I don't care. It grows back.

DESTINY: You know what I want for my birthday? I don't ever want to cut my hair again.

SONIA: Till you trip on it?

DESTINY: Maybe then. Or I'll make a big moño.

SONIA: Beehive, baby.

DESTINY: Like your hair, mami.

(SONIA *laughs.*)

SONIA: Your da looks nice with his short hair. He would look silly if he let his hair grow too long.

DESTINY: Samson had long hair.

SONIA: You got an answer for everything. You get that from me. You're gonna have to cut your hair, papito.

DESTINY: Don't call me that.

SONIA: What if I just trim it? (*She goes to the dresser and pulls out a pair of scissors.*) See?

DESTINY: Not today.

SONIA: Okay. Not today.

DESTINY: Mami?

SONIA: What baby?

DESTINY: You pretty.

SONIA: You're handsome.

DESTINY: I want to be pretty.

(SONIA *stands next to* DESTINY *facing the mirror.*)

SONIA: You see that boy, Danny? That's you. You're like a smaller version of da, and he's handsome, right? You want to be just like him.

DESTINY: I look like you, too.

SONIA: Of course, baby.

DESTINY: Good.

(Living room. ANDY and JORGE are polishing ANDY's work boots. Each has one on their left hand as they polish with their right hand.)

ANDY: Get in there. These boots are old but I can still make them shine like glass.

JORGE: It be easier if I switched hands.

ANDY: What'd you say, Boobie?

JORGE: I'm left handed.

ANDY: It's all in your head. You're right handed. Life is easier if you're right handed.

(Parents bedroom.)

DESTINY: What's your favorite dress, mami?

SONIA: I don't know. I got a lot of favorites. Maybe the red one.

DESTINY: That's my favorite, too.

SONIA: You have a lot of nice clothes, too. I like your little gray suit.

DESTINY: I like how shiny it is. And everybody looks at you when you wear it, mami. You look so beautiful.

SONIA: Do you want to try it on, baby?

(Living room. JORGE keeps polishing.)

ANDY: *(Pointing to a spot on the boot JORGE is polishing)* There. Right there. It's still not good enough.

JORGE: Yes, Mr Andy.

ANDY: I'm already finished with mine.

JORGE: They're your boots. You know them.

ANDY: It's not about knowing them. I finished cause I know what I'm doing. Cause I'm putting some muscle into it. Cause I'm strong. Don't you forget, I'll always be stronger than you.

JORGE: ...Not always, Mr Andy.

(Parents bedroom. SONIA *is holding the red dress. It is indeed beautiful if a bit gaudy. She holds it up against herself and takes a look in the mirror.* DESTINY *is transfixed.)*

SONIA: You want to try it on, don't you?

*(*DESTINY *nods.* SONIA *takes the scissors she was going to use to cut hir hair and cuts into the seam of the dress.)*

DESTINY: Mami!

*(*SONIA, *using all her strength, rips the dress through the seam.)*

DESTINY: Mami don't.

*(*DESTINY *tries to grab the dress.* SONIA *pushes hir who lands on the floor. She continues to cut and rip the dress, throwing what's left of it on the ground. She grabs hir and hugs hir while zie stares at the torn dress on the floor.)*

SONIA: Look at me.

*(*DESTINY *doesn't.* SONIA *grabs hir face roughly in her hand, forcing hir to look at her, then gently kisses hir forehead.)*

SONIA: You are my handsome, perfect son. There will be no dresses for you. Ever. Do you understand me?

DESTINY: ...Yes mami.

SONIA: Mami loves you.

DESTINY: Mami loves me.

SONIA: Da loves you.

DESTINY: Da loves me.

*(*SONIA *picks up the torn dress.)*

SONIA: Stay out of my room, okay papito?

*(*DESTINY *nods. Is about to exit)*

SONIA: Da can't afford to be sad right now. Please don't make him sad, okay?

DESTINY: Okay.

SONIA: That's my good little boy.

(DESTINY *walks out of the room and into the living room where* ANDY *is drinking coffee and* CUCA *is sitting on the floor dressing a doll.* DESTINY *stares at her.*)

ANDY: I like it that you still play with dolls.

CUCA: I'm not playing. I'm imagining.

ANDY: Ah. What are you imagining? Where's she going?

CUCA: To a club. See, that's why I put the dress with the big skirt on it.

ANDY: She can't dance in that thing.

CUCA: Yes she can.

(CUCA *moves the doll around as if it were dancing.* DESTINY *exits.*)

ANDY: Mami and me would go dancing every Friday at the Red Castle. It was a gay club, but it had the best music. I would spin and lift your mother and everybody wanted to be us. (*Laughs*) The men would all hit on me. Your mother got a real kick out of that.

(DESTINY *returns with a toy car, sits on the floor next to* CUCA *and her case of doll clothes and focuses really hard on playing with the toy car.*)

ANDY: What kind of car you got there, Danny?

DESTINY: ...A red one.

CUCA: It's a mustang.

ANDY: Sleek. A muscle car. You want one like that when you grow up?

(SONIA *enters, looks at her family.*)

SONIA: We're eating at the table today. Like a normal family.

CUCA: Not in front of the T V?

ANDY: Who died?

SONIA: C'mon. You too, Danny.

(They all exit, save for DESTINY. *After a beat, zie takes one of the doll dresses and tries to put it on the toy car. It won't go on.)*

(DESTINY goes to hir parents bedroom. Zie lowers hir pants, hir back to us, zie takes Sonia's scissors and holds them at crotch level. Andy enters. Watches his son for a beat.

ANDY: Danny…Danny put the scissors down. …
Please…

DESTINY: *(Whispers)* Destiny… My name is…Destiny.

(Blackout)

END OF ACT ONE

ACT TWO

(From the darkness)

RENE: It's your birthday today, Destiny. We're going to have a tea party. Would you like that?

CUCA: *(Softly)* Danny.

RENE: I'll paint your fingernails and I'll help you comb your hair.

CUCA: Danny.

RENE: You're a very pretty girl.

(Lights slowly begin to come up on DESTINY who is on the sofa. CUCA hovers over hir.)

CUCA: Mami said boys don't faint. I never thought people actually fainted. I thought that just happened in the movies.

(DESTINY sits up.)

CUCA: …It's bad. They were talking so I wouldn't hear. But I did. Did you really try to cut it off?

(ANDY enters with DESTINY's bear and places it next to hir.)

ANDY: *(To CUCA)* Go help mami. She's in your room.

(CUCA exits. ANDY sits next to DESTINY who can't look at him.)

ANDY: You shouldn't play like that. You could have cut yourself, by accident, you know, and we'd have to take you to the hospital, and mami would be crying in the ambulance...

(DESTINY *buries hir face in the teddy bear.*)

ANDY: Nothing happened because nothing's supposed to happen. You're perfect the way you are, you know that right? ...I'm dying, Danny. I don't want to win like this, but it's the truth. I'm very sick. I was trying to shield you, but maybe I was wrong. My balls are killing me and you want to get rid of yours. You're my son. I love you so much. Don't take that away from me. Not now. Please. You can't do this.

(CUCA *and* DESTINY's *former room.* SONIA *is emptying all of hir stuff on to hir bed.* CUCA *stands looking at her mother.*)

SONIA: This is just your room now. All of Danny's stuff goes into the hall closet and the living room, so I can see what he wears and what he plays with. He's not allowed in your room anymore. Does he ever play with your dolls? Do you let him? Cuca, I'm asking you a question.

CUCA: No, mami.

SONIA: You are never to let him touch your things again. Get his stuff out of here. *(Calling out)* Andy!

(CUCA *fills her arms with* DESTINY's *things and heads out.*)

SONIA: Andy, get in here!

(ANDY *and* CUCA *cross each other.*)

DESTINY: Is mami throwing me away?

CUCA: No. But I think you broke her.

(CUCA's *bedroom.*)

ANDY: What are you doing?

SONIA: I need you to put a lock on Cuca's closet door and on all her drawers. Get your toolbox.

ANDY: Mamita.

(ANDY *tries to pull* SONIA *gently by the hand, she pulls away and continues.*)

SONIA: No. I looked the other way for so long. I was gonna let him outgrow it, but no, not now. This is bullshit. This is done as of now.

ANDY: This is not a phase. He wanted to cut his penis off.

(SONIA *stops.*)

ANDY: I didn't dare breathe for a moment. Then I said his name. He stopped and looked at me and said his name was Destiny. He didn't cut into the skin. Not this time.

SONIA: We have to fix him.

ANDY: What if he doesn't want to be fixed?

SONIA: Then he's just gonna suffer his whole life, and you're not gonna be here to protect him. He's not strong enough to be this other person.

ANDY: He was gonna mutilate himself.

SONIA: I'm not stupid! I know that! Help me. I can't carry this family by myself. I'm doing what we need to do. Please, Andy.

ANDY: Okay.

SONIA: We can't be afraid of him hating us for a while. I know who my Danny is. I know what's best for him.

(*Living Room.* DESTINY *hears the sounds of a power drill.* CUCA *drops more of hir things next to hir and exits for more. Zie stares after her. Zie punches the bear who falls to the floor.*)

(RENE *is at the park bench. Enter* DESTINY *dressed like a boy. Zie sits next to her.*)

RENE: You cutting class?

DESTINY: It's gym. It's not a real class. *(Zie puts hir head on* RENE's *shoulder.)* I'll go back before the last bell. I have to.

RENE: What color dress are you wearing?

DESTINY: I'm not. My mami makes me dress like a boy.

RENE: You're still pretty to me.

*(*DESTINY *shakes head "no".)*

RENE: Do they bother you less at school?

DESTINY: They never bothered me that much.

RENE: Your mother wants you to be safe, that's all.

DESTINY: I just want to be happy.

RENE: You'll be happy. Just later on.

DESTINY: Take me home with you.

RENE: So you can play dress up and be surrounded by pretty things? No. That beautiful penthouse with all the servants I told you about, that's not where I live. That was a fantasy. I live in an apartment, over a bodega.

DESTINY: Why did you lie?

RENE: I wanted to make up something. Just like you.

DESTINY: Why did you let me lie?

RENE: Cause you didn't think you were lying.

DESTINY: I'm not hurting anybody.

RENE: No. You're not.

DESTINY: …I don't want my da to die hating me. Do you think he will?

RENE: Is he sick?

DESTINY: Yea. I'm being selfish, right?

RENE: No. He should want to know who you are.

(ANDY *at the punching bag. He can only manage a few punches before he's out of breath.*)

(*Later.* DESTINY *enters* CUCA's *room. There are locks on some of the drawers and there is a lock on the closet door. Zie kicks the door.* SONIA *enters.*)

SONIA: You're not allowed in this room anymore. And I'm taking you to the barber after school.

DESTINY: ...No.

SONIA: It wasn't a question, Danny.

DESTINY: If you cut my hair I'll leave and I'll never come back.

SONIA: I'd find you.

DESTINY: You'd find what's left of me.

SONIA: ...We'll put off the haircut for another time. But you're getting a haircut.

DESTINY: I wish it was you dying instead of da.

(*Later. The moving truck*)

ANDY: You're late.

JORGE: I got left after school.

ANDY: That's not my problem. I gave you a job.

JORGE: I'm sorry.

ANDY: You say you got a family to support.

JORGE: My mother.

ANDY: Then act like it. You're not a boy, you're a man. Put your seat belt on. It's a bitch move. They're just moving around the corner. One no elevator building to another.

JORGE: Where?

ANDY: Staten Island.

JORGE: Why so far?

ANDY: Cause I can't get any jobs here. Cause people can see I'm not the man I used to be. Cause this is a job I used to be able to do on my own and now I need a fat boy who gets himself detention and screws up the little daylight we have left-

(ANDY *begins to hit the steering wheel violently until he is spent.* JORGE *is silent. Looks out his passenger window*)

JORGE: It's safe to pull out now.

(*A still angry* ANDY *goes to adjust the mirror and hits* JORGE *in the nose by accident.*)

ANDY: Oh shit.

(JORGE *grabs his nose. He is bleeding.*)

ANDY: I'm sorry.

(JORGE *nods, holds his nose as blood seeps.*)

ANDY: Wait.

(ANDY *pulls his handkerchief from his pocket and gives it to* JORGE *who leans his head back while holding the handkerchief to his nose.*)

ANDY: ...I'll take you home.

JORGE: No. We're going to Staten Island.

(CUCA *sits at* SONIA's *vanity while her mother combs her hair.*)

SONIA: Your da made one of his guys the foreman. Told him it was so he could run two crews at once. The guy asks him who's he gonna have on his crew. "Don't you worry about that. "I'll get new guys", your da says. The guy says he don't look too good. And POW, your da punches him in the mouth. He gets ready to fight. I mean, he just popped the guy in front of everybody. But the guy looks at him with pity. Your da wants one of them to fight him. Hell, he wants all of them to fight him. But they won't.

(CUCA *looks at* SONIA *who is lost in thought. She sits her mother in her place and stands over her, not knowing how to comfort her.*)

CUCA: Mami?

SONIA: ...Mami's not here. I don't know what to do with the anger, either. I like it better than the sadness, though. Yesterday I snapped at your da in the doctor's office. It was small at first, then I couldn't stop. I started screaming at him in front of everybody. And they're all looking at me like I'm a monster. A nurse comes out to tell me to quiet down and your da just shushes her, and I go warp speed in my rage. I can't form words. I knock over God knows what and run to the bathroom. Hate takes so much outta you. I sit on the floor cause I got no energy left. I disappear. Mami's not here. (*She looks at herself in the mirror.*) Mami's not here.

(*Later.* CUCA *and* JORGE *on the stoop*)

CUCA: I gotta use a key everyday just to dress myself. And Mami checks Danny everyday to make sure he's dressed like a boy.

JORGE: Your mother is losing it.

CUCA: Yeah.

JORGE: She should do what mine does. She sits in front of the T V and drinks and cries. She talks back to the T V.

CUCA: Your mother's losing it, too?

JORGE: No. She's lost it already. I think she hates my father. Or loves him. I can't tell sometimes.

CUCA: You ever see him?

JORGE: Nah. She won't let me. He and his new family are in Florida.

CUCA: It's sunny there.

JORGE: You wanna go sometime?

CUCA: To Florida? How about your mother?

JORGE: Oh yeah. I can't leave her. And how about yours?

(Silence)

CUCA: I dunno. I think she'd be relieved.

JORGE: You want a soda?

CUCA: Nothing is in order anymore. My da was strong and my mother was happy and Danny was pretty.

JORGE: What were you?

CUCA: I was…just me. I was safe.

JORGE: I'll get you a soda.

CUCA: Yeah, okay.

(JORGE gets up to go, kisses CUCA on the cheek. They look at each other.)

CUCA: Do you see stupid written on my face?

JORGE: I don't know. Push your bangs up.

(CUCA punches JORGE, he falls to the ground. He smiles.)

JORGE: It was worth it.

(DESTINY enters wearing a baseball cap. SONIA follows hir. Silence)

SONIA: They didn't take that much off, Danny. I coulda made them give you a buzz cut, but I didn't.

(DESTINY won't look at SONIA.)

SONIA: Okay, you be the parent. What am I supposed to do with you?

(Silence. SONIA exits. DESTINY goes to the punching bag and begins to punch it, harder and harder as he repeats quietly.)

DESTINY: I hate you Danny, I hate you Danny, I hate you Danny.

(ANDY is lit by himself. JORGE appears in the background with an empty dresser on his back. SONIA enters.)

SONIA: You want me to fix you a plate?

ANDY: I ate.

SONIA: I took him to get a haircut. Now he's not talking to me.

ANDY: You knew that was gonna happen. *(He sits in his chair.)*

SONIA: How was the move?

ANDY: *(Laughs)* So I take Boy Boobs on the move with me. Let's see what he's made of. I'm guessing jello.

(SONIA playfully swats ANDY.)

SONIA: Be nice.

ANDY: I'm moving out everything in the living room. Two wing chairs, sofa, tables, lamps. All me. Him, I start him out easy. Give him a boys bedroom set to move out. Twin bed, dresser, night stand. I take him into the room, show him everything he's gotta move. He blinks, swallows, but doesn't say anything. I go to the living room, get my moving straps out, give him a pair. Now you know me, I always start with the heaviest thing first. So after I strap the sofa to my back, it's all about weight distribution, I start for the stairs, and what do I see? He's not using the straps. Boy Boobs has pulled out all the drawers from the dresser, has squeezed his little chubby self into it and is slowly walking the dresser down the stairs. He looks like some wooden turtle. He's moving as slow as one, too. At this rate he won't be done with the bedroom until midnight. But I don't say anything. He takes all day moving that one room of furniture while I do everything else. He never complains. Just keeps going. Huffing and puffing. Grim determination Boy Boobs has. Wouldn't even stop for lunch. When he finally finished, and I'm talking he dismantled every piece he could, carried it down the stairs and reassembled it, he still had to bring down the mattress. I was finished by then. I could have helped him, but I didn't. Boy Boobs just kept moving, one foot in front of the other, until he got the mattress in the truck. He finally looks up at me, wheezing, swimming in his own sweat, his eyes red, I'm thinking he cried a couple of times when I couldn't see him. So he looks up at me and says, "What's next?" Well you missed lunch", I tell him, "but here have half of my Italian sub. And Boy Boobs sat on the curb and ate it. *(Laughs)* God, I hate that kid.

(Later. The bench)

*(*DESTINY, *still wearing the baseball cap, runs in and hugs* RENE, *knocking her book to the ground. She lets the hug continue and slowly returns the embrace.)*

RENE: Oh, Destiny. Sssh.

DESTINY: Mami walks me to school and picks me up at the end of the day.

RENE: She must love you very much.

DESTINY: No, she loves Danny.

RENE: Maybe she loves both of you. Don't you love Danny?

DESTINY: No. I hate seeing pictures of him. I don't like my mother.

RENE: Wait a bit before you decide that, okay? Some things are hard to walk back.

DESTINY: She made me cut my hair.

RENE: Oh. Well, here's my advantage. I only know you from how you described yourself to me. "Dark brown, bouncy, shiny long hair".

DESTINY: I still look like that to you?

RENE: Yes. You should go back to school.

DESTINY: I'm a girl.

RENE: You can be a girl when you're grown. Destiny will always be there, but for now, pick who can see her.

DESTINY: I want everyone to see Destiny.

RENE: Just remember once they do they can't un-see you. You have to really be sure.

(Later. CUCA *and* JORGE *are sitting on the stoop.)*

CUCA: What's it like working for my da?

*(*JORGE *shrugs.)*

CUCA: He treat you nice?

JORGE: Your father calls me boy boobs.

CUCA: To your face?

JORGE: Yeah to my face! When we're in front of other people he calls me B B, but I know what he means.

CUCA: Well, you don't have any, I swear.

JORGE: You would tell me if I did, right?

CUCA: Oh yeah.

JORGE: He's always angry.

CUCA: At you?

JORGE: I don't think so.

CUCA: He's really strong.

JORGE: Yeah, he is. You wanna kiss?

CUCA: Hold up. *(She looks around, kisses him.)*

JORGE: Wait. I was supposed to kiss you.

(SONIA *exits building, is behind* CUCA *and* JORGE. *Watches them)*

CUCA: When did your father leave?

JORGE: Two years ago. My mother's a little crazy now.

(CUCA *kisses* JORGE *again.)*

CUCA: Crazy how?

JORGE: She pulled out all her eyebrows. All. Gone. She looks like a cartoon.

(SONIA *makes her presence known.)*

SONIA: You should go home.

JORGE: I live in the building.

SONIA: Good. Then you won't get lost.

(JORGE *enters building.* SONIA *sits next to* CUCA.)

CUCA: I think I like him, mami.

(SONIA *slaps* CUCA.)

SONIA: What do you know about liking somebody?

(CUCA *runs to enter the building. Then stops)*

CUCA: It's not always all about you, Mami. You can't be mad at everything cause da is dying. I'm not your best girl friend, I'm your daughter, Mami, so act like you know the difference.

(Later)

ANDY: Why you gotta sit in the dark for?

SONIA: I slapped Cuca. Right across the face.

ANDY: Don't you want any of our kids talking to you? She knows what's going on, don't hate on yourself.

SONIA: I pick up Danny from school and I'm the only mother who's child just walks past her, he won't look at me. I'm standing there and I see an express bus

barreling down the street and for just a moment I
thought of jumping in front of it. But I couldn't do it.

ANDY: Cause of the kids.

SONIA: And you. I still love you. I fell in love with you
the second I saw you.

ANDY: Oh I don't think so. You did not like me at all
when we first met. In fact, you hated me. I was moving
you and your family outta your apartment and you
didn't want to go. You sat in your father's recliner and
refused to budge. Everything else was loaded into the
truck and there you were, upstairs glued to that chair. I
moved everything I could until you were the last thing
left, you and that damn recliner. I said, excuse me and
you just ignored me, so I picked up the chair, with you
in it, carried it and you on my back, down six flights.
You were cursing in Spanish most of the way. We get
down to about the second floor and you suddenly
become quiet. That was actually more unnerving. Then
you whispered, "Ain't you tired?"

SONIA: And you said, "Nah. I could carry you forever."

ANDY: I was the strongest man in the world.

SONIA: It's gone. It's all gone.

(Later. Punching bag. CUCA *is throwing punches as*
DESTINY *watches.)*

DESTINY: What's it like having a boyfriend?

CUCA: I don't have a…it's good. He's real nice. He
thinks I'm pretty.

DESTINY: You are pretty.

CUCA: Danny, you never called me pretty before.

DESTINY: When it's just us can you call me Destiny?

CUCA: Why don't you want to be Danny?

DESTINY: I don't know how.

CUCA: You were doing it before.

DESTINY: No I wasn't.

CUCA: Do you hate Danny?

DESTINY: Yeah, cause he's the one mami and da like.

CUCA: I like it when you're Danny.

DESTINY: I'm never Danny.

CUCA: Okay. I will always love you, Destiny. Don't care if you're Danny or Destiny. You wanna be my sister? Okay, you're my sister. And I ain't gonna let anybody hurt you.

(Later. ANDY walks into the CUCA's bedroom.

(Sitting on her bed is Jack the bear, wearing one of CUCA's dresses.)

(Later. SONIA drops off CUCA and DESTINY at school.)

SONIA: I will be back at three. Cuca, check in on Danny after every class. *(She kisses them both.)* Mami loves you.

(SONIA leaves. CUCA takes off her knapsack and hands it to DESTINY. It is pink and flowery. She takes off her colorful belt and puts it on hir. The sisters look at each other. She kisses hir on the cheek.)

CUCA: Meet me back here after the last bell.

(The bench. RENE sits. Enter SONIA, sits by her.)

RENE: Lilacs.

SONIA: What? Oh, it's my soap.

RENE: I know a little girl who smells just like you.

SONIA: He doesn't smell like that anymore.

RENE: I know. Now she smells sad.

SONIA: Excuse you.

(Silence)

RENE: I'm sorry. You're her mother. I'm sure you just want Destiny to be happy.

(SONIA *gets up, speaks as she exits.*)

SONIA: His name is Danny. And he's not gay.

RENE: *(Calling after her)* You're right. Destiny's a girl.

(Later. ANDY *sits on the edge of his bed in his pajamas.* SONIA *enters with the bathroom garbage pail.)*

SONIA: Look what I found in the trash.

ANDY: I don't have to look. It was a bad day.

SONIA: They're soaking wet.

ANDY: I tried to rinse them out. Got depressed, threw them away.

SONIA: These are good work pants. They cost money. Money we don't have anymore.

ANDY: Just leave them! Okay. just leave them.

SONIA: …You have a little accident?

(ANDY *grabs the garbage pail from* SONIA *and throws it on the floor.)*

SONIA: I'm not picking that up.

(JORGE *enters, stands in the back as if he were in the story* ANDY *is about to tell. He has a bottle of water with him.)*

ANDY: I pissed on myself. Can't even control my body anymore. I'm at Auto Zone with Boy Boobs. We're at the counter, waiting for the clerk to bring out my wipers, and suddenly I gotta piss so bad. I know I'm not gonna make it to the bathroom or the door. And I wet myself. All the side of my light gray cotton work pants my piss tracking down in a dark gray. I try to disappear into myself, but… I see the guy coming back with my wipers and I'm standing in a puddle of my own piss. I leave before he reaches me. I stand outside by the truck, sorta dead, you know.

All dignity gone.

(JORGE *opens his water bottle and pours some of it down his pant leg.*)

Boy Boobs comes outta the store and hands me the new wipers. I had forgotten he was standing next to me in the store the whole time. He stayed and paid for them. I can't look at his eyes. Then I see his half empty water bottle and his wet pants. He poured water on himself so he would get blamed for my piss. I put the new blades on and we get into the truck. I'm stinking to high hell in an enclosed cab but Boy Boobs doesn't say a word. Doesn't even crack open a window until he sees me open mine. Now I would have ridden him hard. I'da shamed the boy, tell myself it was all good natured ribbing, but he would have been in tears after I was done with him, I can tell you that for sure. But he, he never said a word. Where does a little punk like that learn something like that, huh?

SONIA: What makes you think he had to learn it?

ANDY: He'll never bring it up, you know. Ever. Not even to Cuca, to let her know her da is....

SONIA: Finish it. Is what? And bear in mind I am itching to slap somebody.

ANDY: He's doing most of the work now. I'm the one who's slowing everything down. I... He's stronger than I am.

(*Later. The bench.* RENE *and* DESTINY.)

DESTINY: Do you have any family?

RENE: I had someone who loved me very much. Her name was Clara.

DESTINY: Not a man?

RENE: No, not a man.

DESTINY: Was she blind, too?

RENE: No, she saw better than most people.

DESTINY: Were your parents okay with that?

(RENE *holds* DESTINY's *hand.*)

RENE: My mother lost herself when I started going blind. I was twelve. Very pretty, too, as I remember; not as pretty as you, but who is? She took me to every doctor she could find. Someone would mention a specialist in another state and we were off. My parents went broke, they divorced. I was totally blind by the time I was fifteen.

DESTINY: Did you cry a lot?

RENE: In the beginning. Mama blamed the universe, God, me, especially when I fell in love with a girl at school. She said, "That's why God punished you, cause you're gay". I almost wanted to let her believe it. She had this exhausted sense of relief to her voice, like she finally got why I was blind, but I told her "There aren't a whole lot of us blind ones, mama. Most of us can see. I'm blind because I'm blind." I know she didn't want me to suffer. Being blind, being gay, she would have taken it all on if it meant I could be happy. She still doesn't get that I was happy with Clara. So happy. Hoo boy, when mama died I'm sure she gave God an earful.

DESTINY: How about Clara? Is she still alive?

RENE: You want me to read you a story? (*She opens her book.*)

DESTINY: No.

RENE: There once was a very beautiful little girl. Named Destiny. But the important part was not how beautiful she was. It was how strong she was. And brave. And although she felt alone, she wasn't.

DESTINY: Could she fly?

RENE: Now you want to fly? She could do anything.

DESTINY: You promise?

RENE: I can't promise many things, but that I can promise. She could do anything. So she went back to her kingdom and made friends with the three bears and let her long hair out the window of a tower and wore a glass slipper and...help me out here.

(DESTINY *closes* RENE's *book.*)

DESTINY: And was very strong.

(DESTINY *kisses* RENE *on the cheek and exits. After a moment,* SONIA *enters, sits, looking after the departing* DESTINY.)

RENE: Hello Lilac Soap.

SONIA: Danny shouldn't be cutting classes. ...He likes you a lot.

RENE: Yes she does.

SONIA: What do you talk about?

RENE: Ask her.

SONIA: ...I'm afraid. I don't know what I'm doing and I'm afraid.

RENE: You want to love her?

SONIA: I don't want to lose my son. I gave birth to a boy.

RENE: You gave birth to a child. I don't have children, but I know it's not easy. And when you're different...

(SONIA *opens her wallet, takes out a picture and goes to show it to* RENE. *She stops herself.*)

SONIA: He's such a handsome little boy. My son. I can't say that anymore, can I? I wish you could see this picture. He's laughing in it. He wasn't always sad. Big smile. I have all these pictures of him I'll have to hide now, because it will upset him. I can't throw them away, so I'll put them under our mattress and when

I'm alone I'll take them out and remember him. I will always miss Danny.

RENE: Take new pictures. Destiny is your child, too. And she needs you. She really does.

(Later. The living room. There is a walker by ANDY's *chair. The punching bag is gone. He sits playing cards with* CUCA. SONIA *is sitting on the sofa painting her nails.)*

CUCA: So then the teacher went to sit and missed the chair and we all had to act like nothing happened and I couldn't look at nobody cause I know I would start laughing.

ANDY: You ain't paying attention to the game. I'm gonna beat you.

CUCA: So the teacher tried to act like she meant to sit on the floor.

ANDY: Gin!

CUCA: I thought we was playing casino.

ANDY: With seven cards?

CUCA: You so stupid.

(Enter DESTINY *wearing hir barrette.* CUCA *takes in her sister,* ANDY *stops shuffling,* SONIA *looks at hir.)*

(She starts blowing on her nails to dry them. There is an awkward silence.)

SONIA: Deal again. That's all. *(She makes space on the couch next to her for Destiny.)* Hey, you want mami to paint your nails?

ANDY: Tomorrow's a school day. Is that a good idea?

*(*SONIA *nods to* ANDY, *smiles at* DESTINY.*)*

SONIA: Pick a color. Destiny.

*(*DESTINY *sits next to* SONIA. *Silence)*

DESTINY: *(Pointing to a color)* I like that one.

SONIA: That's rose blush. Really pretty. Are your hands clean?

(DESTINY *nods.* SONIA *shakes the bottle of nail color, we hear the sound of the ball bearing inside the bottle. She begins applying the nail polish on hir.)*

CUCA: *(Aware of what's happening)* So the teacher sat on the floor for like five minutes.

SONIA: Okay. ...See you gotta do even strokes. I wasn't born knowing how to do it. I had to learn to apply. ...I had to learn...how to apply. You know, when you're home, you can be whoever you want.

DESTINY: Destiny.

SONIA: Yeah, but when you're outside maybe it's probably best to just be Danny.

DESTINY: I can't.

ANDY: Mami just means that it's safer.

DESTINY: So people won't laugh at me, or hate me?

SONIA: Yeah.

DESTINY: So I don't make people angry? *(Silence)* Do I make you angry?

CUCA: You don't make me angry.

SONIA: You don't make me or da angry, either, but can you just be her at home?

DESTINY: No. I'm hir all the time. I can't be anybody else. I don't know how. You want me to hide me and it hurts when I do. It hurts so much. I don't want to hurt you or da, but I know who I am.

SONIA: ...When did you first know?

DESTINY: I always knew.

(Lights shift. JORGE *in the background brings out a wheelchair. He helps* ANDY *get in it and stands behind him.)*

ANDY: I fell in love with Sonia the second she shut up and took my hand. I know what love at first sight is, Boy Boobs, you ain't in love with anybody. Least of all my daughter.

(A small dress shop in the Bronx. SONIA, CUCA, JORGE, ANDY and DESTINY are all there. ANDY is in a wheelchair.)

(DESTINY is wearing jeans and a red tee shirt.)

SONIA: *(To CUCA)* Pick something pretty.

CUCA: You want to pick it with me?

SONIA: No, mamita. You do you. You pick what you like.

CUCA: *(To DESTINY)* C'mon, D. Let's look at dresses.

(CUCA and DESTINY go off to look at party dresses.)

JORGE: Excuse me, Mr Andy.

ANDY: What is it, Boy Boobs?

SONIA: *(To ANDY)* I'ma smack you. So hard.

JORGE: I would like your permission to buy Cuca's dress for her.

ANDY: You ain't buying nothing, B B.

JORGE: Then I'm gonna buy her some flowers.

ANDY: She's fourteen years old, Jorge.

JORGE: And she'll be the prettiest girl at the party. I'll take real good care of her.

(ANDY looks at SONIA.)

ANDY: Find out what color the dress is and make sure it's a flower she likes.

JORGE: Girls like all flowers.

ANDY: See, you're heading right back to being Bob Boobs.

(JORGE turns to leave, stops.)

JORGE: I don't like it when you call me that. Please don't do it again.

(ANDY *stares at* JORGE *for a beat.*)

ANDY: …Yeah. Sure okay.

(JORGE *leaves.*)

ANDY: You'd think I get a pass cause I'm dying.

SONIA: I have a dying husband. I didn't get one.

ANDY: The things that come out of your mouth. I don't hate that boy as much as I used to. But I hate this chair.

SONIA: Yeah.

ANDY: I'm sorry I'm not the man you married.

SONIA: Sssh, papito, it's okay.

(DESTINY *is carrying a few dresses for* CUCA *to try on.*)

ANDY: Hey.

DESTINY: These are for Cuca, dada.

ANDY: All of them? Hold up the pink one.

(DESTINY *does.*)

ANDY: See, I think that would look really nice on you. Why don't you see if they have it in your size? And you can wear it home.

DESTINY: Cause everybody will see me.

ANDY: I'll carry you home on my shoulders, Destiny, and they'll see how pretty you look.

DESTINY: Are you sure?

ANDY: Yeah.

(DESTINY *hugs* ANDY *and runs off with the dresses.*)

(ANDY *turns to* SONIA.)

ANDY: Help me stand.

(SONIA *does.*)

ANDY: Don't look at me that way. I gotta carry her. I've carried all my girls at one point. I carried you, I carried Cuca. I'll do this walk. Even if it's the last goddamn walk I ever do, I'll carry Destiny home. I was the strongest man in the world once.

SONIA: No. Today you're the strongest man in the world.

(Lights slowly fade on ANDY and SONIA and slowly come up on DESTINY, looking at her reflection in the mirror as she wears her new pink dress. Zie stands in the light. Slow fade)

END OF PLAY